A Silver Pen for Cloudy Days

9-23-89

To
Loraine!
Keep "building your
house" with love. May God
bless you as you serve Him.
Susan L. Lenzkes

A Silver Pen for Cloudy Days

SUSAN L. LENZKES

Zondervan Publishing House
Grand Rapids, Michigan

Daybreak Books are published by Zondervan Publishing House
1415 Lake Drive, S.E., Grand Rapids, Michigan 49506

A SILVER PEN FOR CLOUDY DAYS
Copyright © 1987 by Susan L. Lenzkes

Library of Congress Cataloging in Publication Data

Lenzkes, Susan L.
  A silver pen for cloudy days.

  1. Meditations. 2. Lenzkes, Susan L. I. Title.
BV4832.2.L448   1987   242   87-13313
ISBN 0-310-43671-0

Edited by Linda Vanderzalm
Designed by Julie Ackerman Link

Printed in the United States of America

87 88 89 90 91 / AK / 10 9 8 7 6 5 4 3 2 1

To Herb,

and to so many dear friends—
you know who you are—
who have taken my hand
and helped me to trace silver linings
when clouds have been dark.
This book is dedicated to you
because your silver is worth sharing.
Thank you.

*We'd better get used to finding our Lord in the clouds . . .
that's where we are scheduled to meet when He returns.*

S.L.L.

PART I

*Through the Dark Times
God Wants Us
to Learn*

Treasures of Darkness   15
The Shape of a Question   17
Search for the Humor   19
Night Class in Obedience   21
Duty Nags   23
An Emotional Riddle   25
A Circle of Rest   27
The Language of Silence   28
Melting Boredom   31
Saying Goodbye   32
Bound in Misconceptions   34
Time Share   37
Fighting the Real Battles   38
Feeling Insignificant   41
Cutting Remarks   42
Costly Union   43

PART II

*Through the Dark Times
God Wants Us
to Serve*

The Art of the Heart   49
A Friend in Need   50
Ministering Hope   51
Little Lifts   53
Stress Test   55
Lend Me an Ear   57
Hug Power   58
Blanket People   60
Practicing Patience   62
Wise Sayings   63
Love's Cutting Edge   65
A Morning Prayer   66
The Lift of Music   67
Climbing Higher   69
No Small Help   71
The Heart of the Matter   73
No Strings Attached   74
Self-Help   76

PART III

Through the Dark Times
God Wants Us
to Trust

Weathering the Storms   81
He Lit the Darkness   83
One Brief Burst of Glory   85
New Beginnings   87
Pain   89
The Unspeakable   90
In Deep Shadow   93
Just World Furious   95
Pleated Prayers   97
I'm Not Good Enough!   99
Sitting in Darkness   101
To Name a Fear   102
Cultivating Joy   104
Who Betrayed Whom?   107
Teen Trouble   109
The Gift of Laughter   111
Haven on Earth   113
A Lecture to Myself
     at Pruning Season   115
The Morning of Eternity   117

PART IV

Through the Dark Times
God Wants Us
to Grow

Growing Pains   121
You Are Precious   123
Soaring in His Image   125
What a Life   127
God's Exchange System   129
Who's Hurting Now?   131
Choices   133
Don't Give Up!   135
Walking and Waiting   137
Flexible Living   139
A Safe Place   140
The Failure of Failing   143
Resurrecting Dreams   144
A Harvest of Thanksgiving   146
A Tribute to Living   149
He Comes in Winter   151
Today Is Tomorrow   153
Epilogue   155

Acknowledgments

Special thanks to Dr. Al Glenn, professor of Systematic New Testament theology at Bethel Theological Seminary, San Diego Campus, for graciously allowing me to "borrow" the four-point outline from one of his Sunday morning sermons. The sermon, entitled "A Christian Response to Suffering," yielded the division headings for this book, suggesting we are to Learn, Serve, Trust, and Grow through troubled times.

Although I had finished writing this book more than four months before I heard his message, my manuscript fell evenly into its categories like four fingers into a custom-made glove.

Deep appreciation also to my husband, Herb, and to my dear friend Martene Craig for their photographic artistry, which is sprinkled throughout this book. For years we have loved, laughed, and created memories together. Now, some of what we are together is pressed between the pages of this book. I like that.

Finally, thanks to my editor for her efforts, encouragement, and creativity—all designed to make me look good.

PART I

---

*Through
the Dark Times
God Wants Us
to Learn*

Treasures of Darkness

Ye fearful saints, fresh courage take, the clouds ye so much dread are big
with mercy, and shall break in blessings on your head.   William Cowper

Within the depths of
His darkest clouds
God often seems to bury His
richest treasures—
  silver streaks of growth,
  sterling faith,
  precious, gleaming truths—
for His children.

Has a dense cloud of
 doubt,
  pain,
   loss,
    trouble,
     frustration, or
      loneliness
settled over you, dear one?
Search out the treasures of darkness!
The riches of your Heavenly Father hide there—
with your name engraved in silver!

15

"I will give you the treasures of darkness, riches stored in secret places, so that you may know that I am the Lord, the God of Israel who calls you by name." Isaiah 45:3

The Shape of a Question

God is more concerned about what is happening *in* me than what is happening *to* me.
                                                            Gordon R. Bear

*L*ife wasn't going the way it was supposed to go. Like an unruly child, it continued to create trouble and heartache, weighing me down with one of those leaden "why-shaped" question marks hanging around my neck. I walked the question by my husband, hoping for an answer. He had none.

Of my several wise and wonderful friends, at least three can be counted on, in any weather, for an insightful opinion on most any subject, especially if asked. I asked. Not only did they have no opinions, they had no clues. One friend, the one I was positive would have some sort of an answer, whether I liked it or not, said, "I'm as puzzled as you are about this."

Another friend listened as my long string of recent losses shaped itself into its hook-shaped question mark. Then she heard me stab the point to its end as I cried out, "What has God been trying to tell me with all of this?"

"I'm afraid I have no answer for that," she said gently, "but may I pray for you?" And she did, right there on the phone.

It wasn't long after her loving prayer that I began to understand a rule of questioning God. If I'm asking and not seeming to get an answer, perhaps I'm asking the wrong question. Maybe it needs to be rephrased—or redirected.

17

This question needed both. I found it deliberately curving back at me and asking not what God had been telling me but what I had been telling God with my reaction to all that had been happening in my life. Perhaps that I don't trust Him? That He isn't always in control? That I don't believe He's the giver of good gifts? Or that He doesn't really have my best interest at heart?

Put to me like that, I no longer had a question mark but a startlingly pointed exclamation mark. My own attitude was the problem!

It was time to put away the childish measuring stick that insists on using circumstances to test and measure the love and character of God. It was time to reaffirm the truth that God is good, holy, just, sovereign, wise, and that He is Love—pure and beautiful. So I deliberately stopped asking "why" and "what" and began to ask "how."

"How, Lord, are You going to bring good for me and glory for You out of all of this?"

I'm so glad that God's creativity and end results are not limited by His raw materials! I am waiting and watching. I love the way He works—first *in* me, then around me.

> For it is God who works in you to will and to act according to his good purpose.   Philippians 2:13

Search for the Humor

Pleasant words are a honeycomb, sweet to the soul and healing to the bones.   Proverbs 16:24

*I*f there were a gold medal for the woman who's endured the most in unrefined frankness, I'd probably win it.

One day I was propped up in bed keeping my feet warm while I wrote, when my early teen son entered the room and sniffed at the long-stemmed carnation on my dresser, a no-special-reason gift from my sweet daughter.

"Well, it looks pretty, but it sure doesn't smell like much," he commented. And because I never have been able to resist a chance to teach a lesson, I responded, "I know what you mean. Those flowers seem rather like people, don't you think?"

At his surprised look, I went on, "Ever notice how some people look real pretty but don't have very fragrant personalities—like this hothouse flower? But have you ever seen one of those spicy little garden-grown carnations? They may be plain looking, but oh, how beautifully fragrant they are, because their beauty comes from within!"

"Right," he agreed enthusiastically. "Just like you, Mom. You don't look like that much, but you're really a neat person!"

Swallowing hard, I suggested he might want to learn some tact.

"What's tact?" he asked. The question didn't surprise me.

"Well," I said thoughtfully, "it might be easier to explain what tact isn't. And to do that, I'll tell you a story about your Dad when we were first married—before he knew much about tact either.

"I used to want your Dad to think I was pretty, but he apparently had definite and high standards of beauty back then. He had never even hinted that I was beautiful. One night when we were relaxing in front of the fireplace, I teasingly cuddled up to him and said, 'Come on, say you think I'm pretty. You can do it. Just say it, you—are—pretty!' And I wheedled and kidded him until finally he said (in all engineering-personality seriousness, mind you), 'Well, I can't honestly say I think you're pretty. But I *will* say that you do pretty well with what you have to work with!' "

"I get it!" my son burst in. "Then for *tact*, he should have *lied* and said you're pretty!"

Some days a sense of humor is our only shelter from the storm.

It better befits a man to laugh at life than to lament over it.   Seneca

Night Class in Obedience

"He will teach us his ways, so that we may walk in his paths." Isaiah 2:3

*I*t was a bad dream. I woke in tears to find I had been dreaming—as I had so often in daylight—that I could move my strapping teenage son to some cooperative assistance.

The dream began with a friend phoning, announcing her imminent arrival. For whatever reason, the house was in shambles. I hung up the phone and quickly dispensed a plan of action, assigning each family member a separate area of work.

Though all voices assented to the plan, I noticed, as I whirled by doing my own task, that my son still sat, calmly reading the paper.

"Hurry!" I called out. "We don't have much time. He'll be here soon!"

"Oh, sure, Mom," he replied pleasantly, and then casually settled back with the sports page.

A rage of protest welled up in me at such practiced, polite indifference. It was then that I surprised both my husband and myself to wakefulness as my frustration erupted into sobbing.

The next morning I was haunted by the impact of such a familiar slice of real life finding its way into my sleep. Throughout the morning, reason probed my outsized response to such an ordinary aggravation. No amount of surmising or analyzing brought a satisfactory explanation.

Finally, preparing myself to learn some new truth about either me or my son, I prayed, "Lord, if there's something I need to understand from this, teach me."

Suddenly I seemed to hear my Heavenly Father call out, "Children, time is short! I have jobs for each of you!"

I heard myself give easy assent to His instructions—then go on about my business.

"Hurry," He called when He found me idle, "He will be here soon! I have given you a job to which no one else is assigned."

And I responded, pleasantly enough, "Of course, Father," and then went back to my reading.

I sat, stunned at this twist of revelation, and then He went on, "Sometimes you even tell Me, most sincerely, that you *love* Me—right before you go back to your reading. How would you have felt if your son had done that?"

He continued. "My child, it's even worse than that. Your son was only reading the sports page. How deep would your hurt have been if, instead, he were re-reading a very familiar and well-understood list of your urgent instructions for him—searching them for deeper meanings or commenting on their style, form, or accuracy?

"Suppose that when you called out, 'Hurry, there is much to do. Time is short for he is coming!' your child arose but walked right on by the mess to form a group to study your instructions—a group as familiar with them as he? And suppose he expected a reward for this?

"Dear child, listen and truly learn; all the deeper meaning and all reward is found in simple obedience."

Do not merely listen to the word, and so deceive yourselves. Do what it says.   James 1:22

"As long as it is day, we must do the work of him who sent me. Night is coming, when no one can work."   John 9:4

Duty Nags

Duty calls loudest to the hard of hearing.   S.L.L.

I know that my son, the one who hates to pull weeds, has never yet read the entire Bible. He couldn't have, or he would have quoted Ecclesiastes 2:17 by now, claiming biblical backing for the stance that, "work done under the sun is grievous to me. All of it is meaningless, a chasing after the wind."

I sympathize with him. What could be more meaningless than repetitious, lackluster tasks with no challenge and no end in sight? Surely, we were made for better things!

Yet such duties, when ignored, have a way of doubling in duty.

Take my refrigerator, for instance. I save things—bits of this and that— leftovers from a frugal conscience that cannot bear to toss out an edible, no matter how small. Yet, once time has done her hoary duty, my malleable conscience is the first to suggest where garbage belongs. By then, however, the rest of me is resisting involvement.

Cleaning the refrigerator is grievous to me. Not cleaning it is grievous to my husband. How patient he has been! At times he has tackled the job himself. At other times he has waited and won. The other day he approached the whole problem differently.

I came home to find an open refrigerator container with a note attached. The contents were awesome looking—surely high-yield gain in any penicillin lab.

"Success again!" the note exclaimed. "Now, after *many* tests, we have, once again, demonstrated to the world and our outspoken critics that green things can be grown successfully in cold places. Hereafter the need to grow green things in the refrigerator is no longer required. Chief Scientist."

I appreciated the humor. But I could see the truth growing among the green things.

One who is slack in his work is brother to one who destroys.   Proverbs 18:9

An Emotional Riddle

The heart has its reasons which reason does not understand.   Blaise Pascal

What has the power to make small things large and large things small, shy people bold and bold people shy, or bright days dark and dark days bright? A mood!

Moods are colored glasses through which we look at our world. The other morning I got out of bed to an unbelievably gorgeous, sunny day. My mood, however, perhaps in reaction to protracted physical pain, clouded things over considerably. Today the canyons outside my window are being swept with endless brooms of wind-driven rain, and the sky is depression gray. But my own sense of sunshine is back, so I'm free to enjoy the rain.

Through these same tinted spectacles we view ourselves. Occasionally, when I'm about to speak to a group at a banquet or meeting, I experience a wonderful feeling of confidence or ease—even eagerness. Other times, even though I've prepared, prayed, and committed myself in exactly the same way, I fight jitters, concern, and the urge to say, "Why me, Lord? I have nothing worth saying!"

Some moods are like looking through a magnifying lens. Small irritations loom large and can turn ordinary responses into over-sized reactions. Take, for example, the jumble of bookbags, sweatshirts, sportsgear, and shoes that inevitably lands along with

25

my boys' arrival home. Given a certain unfortunate mood, this ordinary clutter gathers itself into a direct and personal attack on my need for order.

So instead of saying, "All right guys, to your rooms with this stuff," I say . . . well, never mind what I say! They wish I'd have spared them, too!

Ranging from wonderful to difficult or downright depressive, moods are a natural response to all that affects us from without and from within—and some days we can't even pinpoint their source!

Mood is simply one of the languages of our emotions and in its native and very primitive tongue, it temporarily suggests the color of our world. We need to learn to say, "This, too, shall pass." For the mist of mood—if indeed it is just mood and not serious depression—scuttles with the winds of time.

We can find comfort in the truth that moods can be managed, lived with in wisdom, and often even used once they are submitted to the control of our Heavenly Father. When we truly give our moods over to Him, He gives them back to us in a way that we can handle.

This knowledge, and the practice of it, promises to brighten any overcast day!

"God understands the way of it."   Job 28:23

A Circle of Rest

Drop thy still dews of quietness till all our striving cease. . . .

John Greenleaf Whittier

Teach me, Lord!
I know I need to learn a lesson
of restraint,
of priorities,
or I would never be this tired.
But teach me, Father,
not from the distance of heaven
nor from behind a pulpit or podium,
but from within Your embrace.
Teach me Your tender love and leading
as I rest on Your
mighty shoulder,
then whisper to me
what I keep forgetting . . .
I must rest within Your arms
constantly
to rest within Your will.

"The Lord, your God, is in your midst . . . He will rest you in His love. . . ."
Zephaniah 3:17 MLB

The Language of Silence

Wisdom often speaks without words.   S. L. L.

I found myself awake in the night, rewriting the script of a fumbled opportunity. Earlier that day I had been in a quiet, unhurried place with a dear friend—obvious opportunity to release the bulging safety valve on pent-up pain over a tragic circumstance that we shared.

But since I had somehow learned to send my pain to charm school, I tried to talk the tears out of my soul in polite little sentences and neatly packaged paragraphs. Now I lay awake acknowledging failure and adding regret to my overload.

Imagination began constructing a second chance. This time I deliberately allowed my questions and my feelings of hurt and loss to speak their own language. I found I was not articulate. There were sudden stops, tear-dampened starts, and halting half-sentences.

Grief's real questions, I realized, have never claimed literacy. Pain and loss are not socialized. Shock stutters. Our deepest feelings are pre-school, even pre-verbal.

Picking up my pen, I shared these fresh understandings with my friend and then added, "As I relived our time together, I finally just imagined myself looking at you—wordlessly and with tears—and you came and hugged me. Wordlessly. With tears. And we held one another's pain without need for explanation.

"I must somehow be overeducated when I cannot set verbiage aside and share feelings properly—naturally. Undereducated is more like it! It has taken me too long to understand that God gifted us with *words* to communicate our *thoughts*. To communicate our *feelings*, He has gifted us with the common language of *tears*, *laughter*, and *touch*. Sometimes words can be an intrusion—an obstacle.

"I'm so grateful that you're in life's classroom with me, my friend, while I learn how to live better, share better, and become more of what I was created to be.

"Making the grade in this class may mean no more than having the integrity to live appropriately, honestly, genuinely, and openly.

"Stick around. One of these days we may have one of our most meaningful conversations without saying a word! And it will be exactly right, for there is surely a pound of encouragement in every ounce of shared silence."

"In quietness and in confidence shall be your strength."   Isaiah 30: 15 KJV

Open my eyes that I may see wonderful things . . . I am a stranger on earth.   Psalm 119:18—19

Melting Boredom

A rut is a grave with the ends knocked out.   Laurence J. Peter

*B*oredom was smothering me in the orange heat of the afternoon when my little boy rushed in with his announcement.

"I know how to catch a moth now, Mommy!" And in demonstration, he stalked, straddle-legged, across the kitchen floor, elbows flung out, hands perched to pounce. "And then you grab him! Like this!" He attacked an innocent spot on the blue tile floor with his powerful five-year-old pincer grip.

"I see," I said, amused. "That looks pretty good. But moths are hard to catch. They have wings—you don't!"

"I can do it, don't worry."

"Well, what if you do catch one?" I continued, determined to confound this seemingly impossible plan. "How will you feed it? What do moths like to eat?"

"Oh, flowers, I guess."

So he spent all afternoon filling plastic sandwich bags with one surprised moth and one small marigold each.

And *I* spent all afternoon learning that boredom is candlewax beneath the flaming wick of discovery and enthusiasm. What a joy to catch the wonder around us, and *in* us!

31

Saying Goodbye

Hearts don't have to stand close to join hands.   S.L.L.

*O*ne of the most heartrending moments of life comes when close friends say goodbye, knowing that many miles will separate them from their countless shared experiences. Distance takes on the menacing look of an enemy when it dares to stand between such friends!

Soon they will find themselves building protective shields around the ache of separation. They will feel themselves both courting and resisting the urge to clip those taut threads that bind their hearts in love. And they will argue repeatedly with a voice that warns, "Don't build new friendships—life has a demolition crew around every corner!"

But discovery lies ahead. Real friendship is resilient. The very cords that made it strong—commitment, creativity, caring, and sharing—are elastic and friends can remain committed and even more creative in their long-distance sharing.

Now cards and letters—stackable memories to be relived over a cup of coffee—will communicate love in indelible ink. Now calls—where the value of every word, enhanced by the coming bill—will set precious priorities and release sentiment from the soul. Anticipated visits will be far richer for their infrequency. Thoughts and feelings long saved and protected will be unlocked and shared.

Best of all, a discovery will be made that hearts in harmony can just as easily carry a tune long distance.

Even though I am not physically present, I am with you in spirit.
1 Corinthians 5:3

Bound in Misconceptions

Watch, therefore, if you think you have life all tied up, lest you trip over trailing misconceptions.   S.L.L.

What daily doings—
          and undoings—
loosen the laces of
          our shiny Sunday shoes of
          certainty about God and His ways?
We learned to tie them—
          so proud—
          over and under, loop around
          and pull tight,
          practicing carefully,
          seeking smiles.

But when life's riddles and pain begin to
          work loose those
          securely tugged knots that assured us
          of a predictable life with God,

And when we trip on our
      trailing laces
      and sit looking at their
      frayed and soiled ends;
and when we can't keep them
      all tied up anymore,
dare we step out of our familiar
      shiny "pat answers" to
      walk on in Truth's barefoot freedom?

For our God is neither
      simple nor manageable,
but He is
      loving and trustworthy.

Stand fast therefore in the liberty wherewith Christ hath made us free, and be not entangled again . . .   Galatians 5:1 KJV

Time Share

We need faith, courage, and lunch together sometime soon.   S.L.L.

A mong God's rich gifts to me are a twenty-four-hour day and dear family and friends. Surely they were given to be spent on one another. But, somehow, that doesn't always happen.

What is it that becomes more important than people? Tasks? Duties? Schedules? Goals? These are ever before us and do claim their rightful hours.

Yet how easily duty becomes greedy! How subtly it taunts us with negligence if we spend time laughing, playing, and sharing with people.

Duty has a way (doesn't it?) of looking more noble than simple sharing with friend or family. Duty manages to sit on a nerve in our conscience and produce guilt if we don't produce, and thus it establishes our time priorities.

So our dear ones wait. And we are all poorer in spirit and character for the lack of touching, helping, lifting, and shaping that we bring to one another.

Of course, duty deserves its proper due, but we need to remember that it dies with us. People don't.

Let us not give up meeting together, as some are in the habit of doing, but let us encourage one another—and all the more as you see the Day approaching.   Hebrews 10:25

Fighting the Real Battles

Fighting the good fight requires fighting the right fight.   S.L.L.

*I*f you're a kitten and you're honing your jungle instincts, everything is suspect. Life requires a constant state of alert. One must be primed, nimble-footed, and ready to bristle and circle at a moment's notice, for things are never as harmless as they seem.

Take, for instance, the day our kitten spied me reading a book on the living room couch and launched a surprise attack from the stairs above. (It took my heart only five or ten minutes to resume its normal rhythm!) Later, he caught my toe moving, pounced on it, and wrestled it into submission.

And what about lethal inanimate objects? Above all, never trust them! They're only playing possum. One day I witnessed our kitten bravely stalk and kill one of my most amenable, non-threatening houseslippers. He didn't even seem to notice that it never fought back. Victory must be in the eye of the aggressor!

I wonder how many battles I've won that weren't a real fight in the first place? How many times have I stalked the corpse of some old forgiven sin, wrestled hard, and then proudly claimed victory?

Perhaps I've pussy-footed around with imaginary threats, bristling at everything. Have I pounced on people who meant me no harm? Do I have a trophy room full of dead houseslippers?

Have I retreated from life's unyielding realities, circled cautiously, then attacked the real with the claws of the ideal?

Has every new movement, anything unfamiliar, seemed a danger to me—something to be disarmed?

Am I neurotically prowling through life playing jungle cat in the midst of real warfare?

When will I learn who my real enemy is? When will I learn the difference between real and imaginary battles?

> For our struggle is not against flesh and blood, but against the rulers, against the authorities, against the powers of this dark world and against the spiritual forces of evil in the heavenly realms. Therefore put on the full armor of God, so that when the day of evil comes, you may be able to stand your ground, and after you have done everything to stand.
>
> Ephesians 6:12–13

Feeling Insignificant

What is man that you are mindful of him . . . ?   Psalm 8:4

> *What awe,*
> *what wonder,*
> *for tiny man on*
> *frail earth*
> *to realize that*
> *size*
> *is no measure of*
> *worth*
> *in God's enormous eyes.*

"Do not be afraid, little flock, for your Father has been pleased to give you
the kingdom."   Luke 12:32

Cutting Remarks

Few are permitted the economy of severe truth . . . only that one who dares stay and minister to its wounds.   S.L.L.

We are often all too eager to perform the surgery of exhortation without taking time to earn the surgeon's license. It takes extensive education and experience to know how to cut someone up to their benefit. Sometimes an operation is advisable, or even urgently needed to save a life. Only in those cases will a caring surgeon advise the patient to surrender to the scalpel and endure the pain. But too many people are performing unnecessary surgery these days. Sometimes it may be due to an error in diagnosis, but at other times the surgery appears to satisfy the one wielding the knife more than it helps the one beneath it.

I need to check both my motives and my license before attempting the quick fix of sharp truth. I may find I'm simply dealing out pokes, digs, cuts, and jabs. Too many of us are hiding scars left by well-intentioned folk impatient with slower, more natural, ways to wholeness—ways costly in time, attention, prayer, and caring.

Needles and knives are safest in the faultless hands of our Great Physician.

. . . If someone is caught in a sin, you who are spiritual should restore him gently. But watch yourself . . .   Galatians 6:1

Costly Union

Man's union was *bought,* while the Godhead's was *split,* at the piercing of
the cross.   S.L.L.

Union, the holy God's union,
invaded by sin's dark clouds.
As lightning cracked death's blackest whip,
the heavens roared forth pain.
And the Father's tears fell.
Oh, the Father's tears fell like rain as
from the cross His Son cried out,
"Father! Why have You forsaken Me?"

Union, God-to-mankind union,
restored through that darkest day.
As lightning cracked sin's leaden veil
the heavens thundered rejoicing.
And the Father's tears fell.
Oh, the Father's tears fell like rain for
from the earth sons and daughters cried out,
"Father! Embrace us, your children!"

Union, love's restored union,
threatened by strife's black clouds.
As lightning trials strike at faith,
God's children thunder questions.
And the Father's tears fall.
Oh, the Father's tears fall like rain for
in their affliction His children cry out,
"Father, You have never forsaken!"

"I have given them the glory that you gave me, that they may be one as we are one: I in them and you in me. May they be brought to complete unity to let the world know that you sent me and have loved them even as you have loved me."   John 17:22—23

PART II

*Through
the Dark Times
God Wants Us
to Serve*

The Art of the Heart

Whoever draws a smile upon a weary soul is God's artist.   S.L.L.

*E*very child born into God's family is called and equipped to be an encourager. God supplies us with the raw materials and challenges us to create and build and shape. For encouragement is one of God's joyous artforms.

Some people combine a helping hand with a word of praise and produce a grateful heart. Others share an absorbent shoulder and a caring ear and spawn fresh perspective.

Often laughter and love have been effectively mixed to paint new sparkle in dulling eyes; belief and support have built self-esteem; persistent prayer composed a song of hope; and tenderness and warm embraces fashioned a friend.

But however we combine the tools of encouragement, one thing we're sure to create is joy—for others, for ourselves, and for our Lord.

I want to be able to do something about your joy: I want to make you happy, not sad.   2 Corinthians 1:24, LB

Therefore encourage one another and build each other up, just as in fact you are doing.   2 Thessalonians 5:11

A Friend in Need

A friend loves at all times, and a brother is born for adversity.

Proverbs 17:17

Friendship gives license to show up at the door of need without asking, "When would you like me to come?" or "What would you like me to do?" Nor does friendship call out, "Just let me know if you need anything."

Practiced friendship whispers, "I'll be there" and promptly steps through the door with sensitivity, respect, and understanding.

But what about honoring the right to invite? Those who wait for parchment invitations wait long, for need rarely throws a party—rarely even has a voice.

Yet need has its own needs. It needs protection from strangers tromping in with work boots and good intentions. And it needs relief from acquaintances wearing the spiked heels of advice and pat answers.

Need waits with longing for the familiar entrance of dear ones who pad barefoot through the soul on ordinary days.

"A despairing man should have the devotion of his friends, even though he forsakes the fear of the Almighty."

Job 6:14

Ministering Hope

The word which God has written on the brow of every man is Hope.
Victor Hugo

*T*he first word to wither and drop from the vocabulary of the discouraged is *hope*. And even if God has written HOPE on my forehead, I find that I'm still in trouble. For reading my own forehead is about as easy as kissing my elbow.

Then those who mirror the love of God come to me, and I see Hope reflected in their eyes. And that Hope, I discover, is not a thing, but a person—the person of Jesus Christ.

So they bring Christ to me through a helping hand, a word of encouragement, a message of love, and a touch that heals. Through such ministrations, they have stretched my small soul to receive the great Hope.

Christ always ministered like this—stretching shrunken souls with acts of love and compassion before imparting the large Truth of Who He was. And still today He is not content to settle back in the easy chair of our affection. He longs to go on ministering Hope through us.

Blessed be the God and Father of our Lord Jesus Christ who according to His ample mercy has given us new birth into a life of hope, through the resurrection of Jesus Christ from the dead. . . .   1 Peter 1:3 MLB

Little Lifts

The size of a deed is measured not so much by its effort as by its impact.

S.L.L.

My husband, an early riser, often wakens me, a night owl, by placing a steaming mug of coffee on my nightstand. Such a small thing, but it makes me feel so cherished and pampered!

A friend regularly jots me a note of love, appreciation, or encouragement. How can one thin piece of paper lift me so high?

Another friend makes a quick phone call that manages to warm my whole day. My son passes by and stops to rub the weariness from my shoulders, and this time he doesn't even want anything! A neighbor calls out a cheery greeting that lingers. A stranger passing on the sidewalk dares to look me in the eyes and smile.

A brother from church sees me carrying a heavy load and says, "Here, let me." A "hello" comes enveloped in a hug.

Someone says, "You look wonderful in that color" or "What you shared helped me" or "I missed you yesterday" or "I was praying for you this morning" or "Come share my sandwich."

Someone gifts me with a contagious laugh; a toddler shyly presses a damp M & M into my hand; my daughter shares a secret; someone unexpected remembers my birthday with a card and note; a friend calls and says, "Quick, go look at the sunset"; my sister touches my hand with unspoken understanding; a friend says, "Try again, I know you can do it."

These are the things that brighten and lighten life. These are the little things that make a big difference. They're not expensive, difficult, or time consuming. They're just appreciated, remembered, and so vitally important. They're each day's small building blocks of love.

"Who despises the day of small things?"   Zechariah 4:10

Stress Test

Many are they that rise up against me.   Psalm 3: 1 KJV

*I*t happened several years ago, but I can still remember the feel of that moment as I stood in the family room, agitated and bundled in my coat.

It had been another one of those days—the kind when you can't remember which interruption is being interrupted. But most memorably, it had been one of those days when everybody had been breaking off pieces of me, and someone had just snapped the last straw—that last little piece holding this wife/mother/friend/church-worker together.

My husband sat observing me from the couch. "And just where do you think you're going?" he asked.

Arms slicing the air for emphasis, I announced that I didn't know and didn't care, but that it was definitely going to be someplace remote and undemanding. "Everybody expects too much of me!" I concluded, marching to the closet for my purse.

My husband's irritatingly calm voice followed me, "I hope you don't plan to run too far. I really don't think that car could make it much beyond forty miles in its present condition."

Yanking off my coat, I hurled it to the floor and burst into tears. "Just what are you supposed to do when you can't run away?"

I soon found out.

When I realized the car wouldn't make it, and neither would I, I knew it was time to stay home and examine why I felt so drained, so spent, so empty. I began to discover that we have choices, that we are helpless victims of demanding circumstances only if we choose to be!

We will always face the pressures of jobs, schedules, deadlines, finances, pain, illness, disorganization, interruptions, noise, clocks, change, crisis, and relational difficulties with spouse, children, neighbors, friends, or co-workers. These pressures turn to destructive stress only when they collide with our own bad attitudes of inflexibility or inadequacy or with our lack of acceptance, humor, trust, or creativity. We choose our own attitudes.

We also choose our priorities. As we search out God's priorities for us and say "no" without guilt and "yes" without reservation, we catch hold of the enormous truth that *people cannot take from us what we freely give away.* Finally we discover the miracle of servant-living.

This, then, is how we give ourselves away without coming apart. It is the lesson of the cross.

"The reason my Father loves me is that I lay down my life—only to take it up again. No one takes it from me, but I lay it down of my own accord."
John 10:17–18

Lend Me an Ear

It is impossible to over-emphasize the immense need humans have to be really listened to.   Paul Tournier

For every person in need of a listening ear, there will be dozens with something burning on the stove.   S. L. L.

A listening, caring, available ear is exceedingly difficult to find. Ears are busy these days. Many seem permanently encased in the headphones of their own private interests. Some have been upstaged by other parts of the body—such as an eye on the clock or a nose to the grindstone.

And even a free ear isn't necessarily free just to listen. When people come to us with their troubles, many of us discover a birth defect—our earbone is connected to our mouthbone. And so a mixture of advice, platitudes, and an "experience to top *that*" flows forth.

The burdened who come to us needing to unburden are looking for an earbone connected to a *heartbone*.

He who has an ear, let him hear.   Revelation 13:9

Hug Power

If a hug can't help it, call in a specialist.   S.L.L.

*I*f someone started selling stock in hugs, I'd mortgage my house and go for it.

Hugs are indispensable. They're the shape of a full heart, the feel of love. They're as useful in good times as they are in bad (they're as good at celebrating as they are at comforting!). And notice how they're used as freely in greetings as in farewells . . . not to mention all the times in between!

Hug experts even claim that people must have a minimum daily requirement of hugs for the maintenance of health and sanity. Sounds right to me! I credit hugs with great power.

I tell myself that hugs speak wordless love, transliterated to perfection according to the need of the one I hug. (Actually, it's that I don't know my heart's vocabulary and my precocious arms are claiming linguistic degrees.)

I like hugs because they briefly squeeze shut the space between hearts. For a moment our aloneness is wrapped about with someone else . . . a blanket against isolation.

But a hug is especially valuable in times of trouble. On some days it seems that a friend's gentle understanding hug is the only added pressure the wounded heart can bear.

Taking him [a little child] in his arms, he said to them [his disciples], "Whoever welcomes one of these little children in my name welcomes me; and whoever welcomes me does not welcome me but the one who sent me."   Mark 9:36—37

Blanket People

The shivering soul seeks a blanket of love.   S.L.L.

This dear couple, Lord,
is like a cozy afghan
on a cool evening.
One has the wisdom of wool,
the other, warm color—
rich design.
I search for them when I'm
chilled,
and somehow with just a look,
a word, or a hug,
they wrap themselves snugly
about my heart.
I know now how it feels
to be embraced by You.

S ome days we're burdened with such an inflated sense of failure and exhaustion that we cannot imagine even God's arms opening wide enough to hold the expanse of us! We sit alone in the chill of our shortcomings and read in God's Word that Jesus said, "Come to me, all you who are weary and burdened."

Yet we cannot allow ourselves to experience the engulfing stretch of His arms as He opened them on the cross . . . until a blanket person wraps us in acceptance and love by choosing to be near us when we would not even choose to be near ourselves.

God needs His blanket people, each with their unique color and design, each a demonstration of His warm, enfolding love.

Also, on a cold night, two under the same blanket gain warmth from each other, but how can one be warm alone?   Ecclesiastes 4:11 LB

Practicing Patience

The greatest thing a man can do for his heavenly Father is to be kind to some of his other children.
                                                            Henry Drummond

*T*he little boy didn't seem to know or care that he'd wandered into the intersection. He was preoccupied with dangling a palm branch just beyond the toe of each step—a tantalizing target designed to see if his feet could outsmart his hands. The driver who'd been forced to stop in the middle of the intersection and wait out this tedious trek turned toward my car, knowing he was blocking my passage, and threw his hands up in resignation and his head back in laughter.

Dear man, I thought, joining him in laughter, *bless you for your watchfulness, patience, and sense of humor that allows you to help this little one survive his walk home—and even enjoy him.* And I thought about all of God's children on their way home: some so young they don't know how to safely cross the street; some rushing and bumping into others; some wounded and running blindly into life's intersections; and some just distracted, preoccupied, playing little games with their feet. How pleasing to the Lord are those willing to brake for the progress of His children—and even smile about it.

Take tender care of those who are weak and be patient with everyone.
                                                            1 Thessalonians 5:14 LB

Wise Sayings

May all the wonderful things I will say about you after you are gone be found, complete, in the thesaurus of our todays.   S.L.L.

The grief of loss is a heavy load. Pity those who find themselves adding regret to its burden. The "if onlys" can tip the scales and unbalance us if we're not careful.

With each new day God offers us opportunities to prevent regret. Today we can speak encouragement, voice our feelings. If we do it now and say it now, we are practicing the wisdom of kindness.

I have long held a motto that if I think a kind thought about someone—anything at all—and do not pass it on, I am wasting diamonds. Yet, regrettably, I find I have wastecans filled with diamonds. The kind thoughts that form in us, yet are never shaped into words or acts, may prove to be the squandering of our most valuable human resource.

Today let me tell you, my friend, that your laugh is as much fun for me as it is for you—that your tears land in my heart—that tea with you is always sweeter—and that knowing you are there for me feels like owning the national treasury.

Today let me say, my child, that I see greatness in you—that I love seeing life through your eyes—that you are growing evidence of God's goodness to me—and that sometimes I sneak in and watch you sleep and can't help congratulating myself!

Today let me tell you, my husband, that every time I pray for you my prayers turn into praise—that your weariness, frustrations, and joys are mine—that you have wonderful hands—and that your steady, faithful character is the most beautiful love letter ever written.

Today let me say to you, my parents, that I'm glad you had me and even "gladder" that I had you; that I loved taking my husband's name but hated giving up the name that linked me with you; that I lean on your love, count on your prayers, and live on your lessons; and that the twinkle in your eyes when you look at one another ought to be patented!

Today let me tell you, my Heavenly Father, that I am rich because of You— that I stand in awe of Your creativity every time I give You one of my tangled messes—that You are Altogether Beautiful—and that I love the family You are building for Yourself. Thank you for letting me be part of it!

A word aptly spoken is like apples of gold in settings of silver.
Proverbs 25:11

Love's Cutting Edge

Hugs are delightful—until you meet a porcupine! S. L. L.

*H*ow many of us struggle to find ways to embrace "porcupine people!" They can be relatives, neighbors, or co-workers, who bristle at the slightest provocation, who needle us constantly and dish out sharp digs and stabs. Any attempt to reach out or come close can be a wounding experience. Yet dare we stop trying?

The "porcupines" in our lives need love far more than other people. Their rigid quills often cover startlingly low self-esteem and deep personal wounds and pain.

It will cost us some of our own blood and tears to get close enough to hug off the prickles. But can we claim to pick up our cross and follow Christ without sharing His crown of thorns?

But rejoice that you participated in the sufferings of Christ, so that you may be overjoyed when his glory is revealed. . . . So then, those who suffer according to God's will should commit themselves to their faithful Creator and continue to do good. 1 Peter 4:13, 19

A Morning Prayer

My most unselfish act may be to pray first for myself.   S.L.L.

Jesus, forgive me
for the selfishness
of hurt feelings
and insensitivity
to the needs
of those around me.
Give me Your
keen sight and hearing
to know just where to spread
the healing ointment
of Your love.
Please provide a supply
just right for today.
And Lord, tie a string
around my heart
reminding me that
this is Your day, not mine.

Therefore, as we have opportunity, let us do good to all people, especially to those who belong to the family of believers.   Galatians 6:10

66

The Lift of Music

When words leave off, music begins.   Heinrich Heine

A bumper sticker on the back of my car claims "Without music, life would be a mistake." It was given to me by a dear friend, one who knows what the gift of song has meant in my life, one who has blended her beautiful heart and voice with me, and with another precious friend, to minister through music.

It's impossible for me to dissect or fully explain music's ways. I have no real knowledge of the varying lengths or patterns of sound waves or of their effect on the vibrations of the human ear. But I do have some understanding of its impact on the human heart, for music seems to be the heart's native tongue.

How often I have sat cross-legged between the speakers of my stereo, singing or just letting music wrap itself about my wounds and weariness. How often I have dragged myself to a rehearsal or performance and have come away restored. Music has power to lift, speak, soothe, teach, touch, energize, and unify.

Melody adds wings to words and sails them past all obstacles. Its practiced fingers are able to reach isolated souls and pry loose spirits long boarded over.

Music carries within its measures a large measure of comprehension. Somehow we can believe love that serenades us. Somehow we can hear hope that sings back to us in the dark.

67

Yet, even if music could do none of these things, if music gave voice to our praise, it would still confirm the message of that bumper sticker. For without voice or melody to praise our Redeemer, this life would be sadly amiss!

Begin the music . . .   Psalm 81:2

. . . Declare the praises of him who called you out of darkness into his wonderful light.   1 Peter 2:9

Climbing Higher

If God intended children to drive us up the wall, He would have created
suction cups on the bottom of our feet.   S.L.L.

P arenting is a high and holy calling, came the pronouncement from the pulpit.
"High and holy calling, indeed," I muttered, slumping back in my seat. "High
because they have us climbing the walls half the time, and holy because they use us for
target practice!"

I had, in fact, arrived at that service late—just in time to hear the choir sing
without me—precisely because of my parental calling. My youngest had been
practicing outrageous defiance in an assumed "safe zone"—he knew Mom needed to be
somewhere else. But fresh understanding of my priorities dawned in his eyes as our car
turned for home and he anticipated the private lesson that was about to be impressed
upon his, ah . . . mind.

It doesn't help to romanticize the often rugged call of parenting. It does help to
pray that we stay tough. And when we do find ourselves as high as the ceiling, it helps
to look up still farther until we have a perspective as high and holy as our Lord's.

Let us run with endurance the race that is set before us. . . . fixing our eyes
on Jesus.   Hebrews 12: 1–2 NASB

No Small Help

Don't let us think that we need to be "stars" in order to shine. It was by the
ministry of a candle that the woman recovered her lost piece of silver.

John Henry Jowett

I had just been unceremoniously informed of my shortcomings as a mother. My thwarted and angry preteen had drawn on the full lexicon of his experience and vocabulary to perform the task. His awesome barrage of accusations somehow managed to penetrate my shield of better judgment. I sat nursing wounds in my bedroom and wondering if I might, indeed, somehow hail from the family tree of Frankenstein.

Soon I heard footsteps, both tentative and rushing. The folded paper thrust into my hand was accompanied by only the briefest look into my eyes—a glance of shy, quick compassion—before this youngest son ran back out of the room. He had been a silent witness to my Waterloo with his brother.

I looked down at the paper. "To a great mums!" it read. (He has never called me mums before or since.) Tenderly I unfolded his message and read (creative spelling and all), "I am glad you are my mums because you help me and care for me and show me how to eat the right way." (He did say only that I'd shown him; he didn't claim that he'd learned!) "You rote a book for mothers who need help" (In which case, I wrote the book for myself!) "and rote the book for money to help us live." (Fortunately, that wasn't my motive!) "You help mothers because you care for others and not onley for yourself. So that proves that your the perfecked mother for just about anyone. Love, Matt, Your Son." (No extra charge for the identification!)

At the bottom of the page was a wonderful drawing of a skinny stick person with long arms stretched out to a typewriter, presumably working on a book to help others—so she could live off the proceeds!

Is there anyone too small or weak to lift sagging spirits with a heartfelt message of love and faith?

From the lips of children and infants . . .   Psalm 8:2

An anxious heart weighs a man [or a woman] down, but a kind word cheers him [or her] up.   Proverbs 12:25

The Heart of the Matter

The real danger is not that computers will begin to think like men, but that men will begin to think like computers.   Sydney J. Harris

Some people worry about being replaced by a computer. Mothers never hold such a worry . . . they don't even hold such a hope!

What self-respecting computer would be caught rinsing a diaper in a toilet? No computer has a program for such lackluster tasks as mopping spills, folding undershirts, or scrubbing baked-on lasagna. A computer might be helpful in repeating such endless and wearisome commands as "close the door," "wash your hands," and "don't hit your sister." But it would have no firm hand to aid the learning process. We might find a computer helpful in organizing lists of duties for ourselves and our children. But computerized lists don't cajole, encourage, or praise.

Computers can say "thank you," but they can't smile when they say it. They can declare "it'll be okay," but they can't wipe away the tears. They can exclaim "you're wonderful," but they cannot confirm it with a warm hug.

Love can never be transistorized!

We continually remember before our God and Father . . . your labor prompted by love. . . .   2 Thessalonians 1:3

73

No Strings Attached

Beware the one who serves his own needs by claiming to serve yours.
S.L.L.

I t was one of those rare, luxurious wake-up-at-your-own-pace Saturday mornings. My husband and I were taking full advantage, stretching and purring like cats on a hearth, when our fourteen-year-old son joined us, piling on top of his dad's back.

Eventually I heard my husband say, and it was quite obviously directed to his piggy-backer, "A cup of coffee sure does sound good!"

"Sure does!" I agreed enthusiastically. Our son began a loud protest. "Oh, no, you guys are just trying to put a guilt trip on me! I don't want to make you coffee!"

"Well, we were just saying it would be *good*," his dad reiterated.

"Sounds pretty straightforward to me," I observed. "Besides," I went on, beginning to wake up to the fun of it, "didn't Jesus say it's more blessed to give than to receive? We're just trying to get you *blessed!*"

"That's right," my husband joined in, "we're only doing this for *you!*"

"All right, all right, I'll get your coffee!" he yelled, jumping up and rushing out. "You guys are the *major* guilt-trippers!"

Wide-eyed with feigned innocence, my husband and I looked at one another, asking how on earth he could think such a thing. Then we giggled—two successful conspirators.

Fun stuff—when it's deliberately light-hearted and everyone's playing the game. Trouble is, real manipulation is accomplished subtly, regularly, and with serious consequence.

Manipulation, well done, gets us what we want, but at the expense of another person's freedom to choose. "You *owe* me . . . ," "But haven't you always *said* . . . ," "How *could* you, after all I've done . . . ," "Everyone *else* knows that . . . ," "God's *Word* says you have to . . . ," "If you really *loved* me . . . ," "Don't you *trust* me . . . ," "Someday when I'm *gone* . . . ," and so on.

Sometimes we don't even need words. Often a wounded look, a sigh of disappointment, or an authoritarian glare serve just as well.

If we're going to be completely honest, we'll have to admit that manipulation is a relational cancer. And when we practice its coercion, we are diseased people.

Another honest look tells us that those who allow themselves to *be* manipulated are feeding the cancer—contributing to the sickness. Fresh reason for practicing a firm "no" or learning to withdraw from the clutches of a conniver, whether acquaintance, family member, or friend.

At great personal expense, God gifted us with the freedom of choice. The bold manipulator dares to live out this message: "The Lord giveth, *I* take away!"

> You . . . were called to be free. But do not use your freedom to indulge the sinful nature; rather, serve one another in love.   Galatians 5:13

Self-Help

It is one of the most beautiful compensations of this life that no man can seriously help another without helping himself.   Ralph Waldo Emerson

When I lift you, my friend,
my arm grows stronger.
When I give to you,
my hand empties to receive.
When I walk with you through
dark valleys,
my feet learn the way to Truth.
When I weep with you,
my eyes wash clear to see
compassion's holy bond.
When I lift you,
I am lifted.

"In everything I did, I showed you that by this kind of hard work we must help the weak, remembering the words the Lord Jesus himself said: 'It is more blessed to give than to receive.'"   Acts 20:35

He who refreshes others will himself be refreshed.

Proverbs 11:25

PART III

*Through
the Dark Times
God Wants Us
to Trust*

Weathering the Storms

Without the rain, God couldn't parenthesize certain moments with rain-bows.

S.L.L.

Oh, Lord,
let this trouble,
this trial,
cause me to be
still
and know that You are
God.
Use this tension as
surface tension to
hold me,
clinging like a droplet
after a storm,
patiently suspended,
yet holding fast to my
Vine of Life.

*T*he storm swirled, throbbing about my little car as it headed toward the dark mountains. As nature staged the hidden tempest in my soul, my hand moved in rhythm with the windshield wipers doggedly slashing at sliding drops.

Lightning and heartbreak stabbed in jagged flashes. Thunder roared. Leaves and questions tossed wet in the wind.

The torrent poured on before me, yet the sun began to touch and warm my back. A rainbow, soft and wide, embraced the darkest mountain top. "Lo, I am with you always. I promise, my child. I promise!"

So beautifully God paints understanding and peace with strokes from His own rich palette of promises.

> *God is our refuge and strength,*
> *an ever present help in trouble.*
> *Therefore we will not fear, though the earth give way*
> *and the mountains fall into the heart of the sea,*
> *though its waters roar and foam*
> *and the mountains quake with their surging.*
>
> *Psalm 46:1–3*

He Lit the Darkness

The people living in darkness have seen a great light; on those living in the land of the shadow of death a light has dawned.   Matthew 4:16

What was December 25th
before it was Christmas?
Just a chilly day
twenty-five sighs into an
endless winter night.
But when it became Christmas—
oh, when it became Christmas
it glowed!

A star, radiant and compelling, announced Christ's birth. Yet to those who found the Babe beneath its beam, it must have paled to a mere spark. For what was that dazzling ball of fire compared to God's million-watt Gift, the resplendent miracle of the ages? God had poured all of Himself into dimpled arms and legs. Then, with His first cry; He lit the darkness of an old stable and of a whole lost world. For His was the brilliant cry of salvation!

This is how God showed his love among us: He sent his one and only Son into the world that we might live through him.   1 John 4:9

One Brief Burst of Glory

Heaven gives its favorites—early death.   George Gordon

Like an annual flower,
*   she blossomed*
in one brief burst of glory,
*   dazzling eye and heart.*
Designed by her Creator
*   for one treasured season of*
joy and inspiration—
*   then gone—*
never needing to know
*   cruel pruning shears*
nor harsh, barren winters
*   and painful, repeated struggles*
up through frozen sod to
*   gray and weeping skies,*
as we perennials must.

Precious in the sight of the Lord is the death of his saints.   Psalm 116:15

New Beginnings

The best thing about the future is that it comes only one day at a time.
Abraham Lincoln

The beginning of a new year—always an experience in tentative hope! Those midnight chimes that ring out the old year and bring in the new seem to chant, "What lies ahead?" And feeling both fear and trust within us we grope to join hands in fortress against the unknown. Secret dreads worry away the edges of new chances. Precious ties whisper their fragility. Clocks tick ever faster.

Yet pushing up through our apprehension like a crocus through snow is the bright delight of opportunity. For there sits that calendar, fresh and yawning to be filled with dreams achieved and goals attained. And there stands our Lord saying, "Fear not, just follow Me. I am the same yesterday, today, and forever."

When times are good, be happy; but when times are bad, consider: God has made the one as well as the other. Therefore, a man cannot discover anything about his future.
Ecclesiastes 7:14

But I trust in you, O Lord. I say, "You are my God." My times are in your hands. . . .
Psalm 31:14—15

Pain

He has seen but half the universe who never has been shewn the house of
Pain.   Ralph Waldo Emerson

> *My life is*
> *Your song, dear Lord.*
> *And if You choose to*
> *write that song,*
> *in part,*
> *in minor key,*
> *give voice to sing above*
> *the salty taste of tears.*
> *With hands hard-clasped*
> *in pain*
> *and head bowed low*
> *in trust,*
> *I know You hear such*
> *minor songs*
> *as major praise.*

My eyes are ever on the Lord, for only he will release my feet from the
snare. Turn to me and be gracious to me, for I am lonely and afflicted. The
troubles of my heart have multiplied; free me from my anguish.
                                                    Psalm 25:15—17

The Unspeakable

Compassion invites the honesty that voices the unspeakable and brings healing.   S. L. L.

I had been caring for little Stevie and was calling for him—just checking— when I heard his voice respond, remote and subdued. Following the sound downstairs to a corner of the living room, I found him on the floor, kicking at the bottom of an easy chair and biting at his lower lip.

Clearly he had sought this lonely spot to deal with distress heavier than a three-year-old boy knew how to carry. As I knelt beside him and touched his shoulder, I watched pride battling for control in his face.

"What's the matter, Stevie?" I asked. "You seem so sad."

He turned toward the chair, covering his face with his hands, and I thought that this little one who laughed and hugged so easily was going to shut me out from his hurt. But then, with large wet-lashed eyes, he turned and looked at me. "I'm mad with mommy," he whispered, almost inaudibly.

"You're angry with your mommy?"

"Yes. She keeps going away. She always goes away to the hospital to be with my sister, 'cause Katy's sick. But I don't *want* her to." He drew in a deep, shaky breath. "It's not good," he concluded. "It's not good for mommy!"

"No," I agreed gently, "and not good for Stevie either, is it?"

"No, not good for Stevie either," he admitted, and then he wept without restraint.

I gathered him into my arms, rocked and kissed him, and whispered that I knew he felt so sad. I told him how special he was and how much his mommy missed him when she had to be away to help his baby sister get over her bad sickness.

It was then, as we snuggled together, that I found myself remembering the time, months earlier, when *I* had felt this way.

My precious friend had been sick with cancer. The knowledge of it had placed an angry, malignant sorrow within me. Wasn't she God's faithful, loving, and fruitful servant? Didn't the world need her? And, oh, didn't *I* need her?

So I, too, withdrew to a lonely spot, biting my lip for control, trying to hide. But I was hiding from *God*, for I was angry with my Lord Who had the power to prevent it—but hadn't.

He found me, though, and then urged me, helped me to cry out my rage, frustration, and indignation. At His gentle yet insistent probing, prayers too wounded to couch themselves in acceptable, respectable phraseology cried out, "Unfair!" And even the unspeakable, "Yes, I am angry with You!" And I wept, then, without restraint, feeling that He should surely strike me down.

But as I cradled Stevie in my arms, I remembered that day and understood afresh that God is our Father of intimate, loving compassion. And such compassion never reacts; it responds . . . invites . . . enfolds . . . no matter what we're feeling or trying to hide.

If I discovered no neat little wrapped-and-tied answers that day, I did find release, peace, and unspeakable rest in the tender sovereignty of such a God.

The Lord has heard my weeping. . . . the Lord accepts my prayer.
Psalm 6:8–9

It's all right
questions, pain, and
stabbing anger
can be poured out to
the Infinite One and
He will not be damaged.
Our wounded ragings will be
lost in Him and
we
will
be
found.
For we beat on His chest
from within
the circle of His arms.

I cry aloud to the Lord . . . I pour out my complaint before him.
Psalm 142:1–2

In Deep Shadow

"We look for light, but all is darkness; for brightness, but we walk in deep
shadows."   Isaiah 59:9

Dear child of God,
when clouds descend,
when depression wraps its
heavy cloak about your soul,
when God seems distant and
you, so alone—
stretch out a finger of faith,
for you may be closer than you've
ever been . . .
He may be hiding you in the
shadow of His wing.
Beneath God's wing
deep shadow blocks our sight
and bids us hear our
darkest feelings whisper
their pain, loss, and unmet needs
into the sufficiency of God's love.

He who dwells in the shelter of the Most High will rest in the shadow of the Almighty. . . . He will cover you with his feathers, and under his wings you will find refuge. . . .

Psalm 91:1—4

". . . the Lord will be your everlasting light, and your days of sorrow will end."

Isaiah 60:20

Just World Furious

When the storm has swept by, the wicked are gone, but the righteous
stand firm forever.   Proverbs 10:25

*E*very now and then we ought to check the shoulders of our young to see what adult-sized burdens they are carrying—what responsibilities, what pain, and what fury they have gathered upon their inexperienced slopes.

My youngest son was struggling under a weight that would have staggered even the most seasoned adult. He was, quite literally, carrying the weight of the world. And I might never have known that the heavy realities and injustices of this world were settling in on him if he had not been told to write a small booklet of poems for one of his grade-school classes.

Among lighthearted poems about himself and his grasp of life, came this one called, "Just World Furious."

> *I'm furious.*
> *Not just beat-up-someone furious,*
> *Not go-rip-up-my-room furious,*
> *Not furious like a man who lost*
> *His job and he's going to commit*

Harry carry.
But just furious with the world
Because of what it owns,
Furious because people kill each
Other,
Furious because people steal
Money and commit robberies,
Furious because I can't do
Anything about these awful deeds.

"Furious with the world because of what it owns . . ." Me too, dear son, me too. It is a terrible combination of woes to see the injustices of evil at the same time that we see our own helplessness to right its wrongs.

But for the Christian, and through the Christian, there is hope. We are instructed to be salt—seasoning, purifying, preserving salt; and light—revealing, beckoning, healing light. And we are instructed to spread the Good News that there is One in Whom justice dwells—One Who has won the final victory over this world at the battle of Calvary.

We are simply on the stage with Evil's closing act. This brings us both grief and opportunity.

> Be very careful, then, how you live—not as unwise but as wise, making the most of every opportunity, because the days are evil.   Ephesians 5:15–16

[Poem, "Just World Furious," used by permission of Matt Lenzkes.]

Pleated Prayers

Prayer is the soul's sincere desire, Uttered or unexpressed; The motion of a hidden fire That trembles in the breast.   James Montgomery

Her eyes are homes of silent prayer.   Alfred, Lord Tennyson

> *Never-ending "pleated prayers"—*
> *rich fabric of a loving heart—*
> *hope folded,*
> *endlessly folded,*
> *over tear stains,*
> *and wrapped like a skirt around*
> *the throne of God.*

I t crowds reason and logic to imagine constant prayer. "Pray without ceasing," God commands. We realize this is important, but how on this earth—with all its schedules, demands, and distractions—do we *do* it?

I once told a hurting friend that I was holding her in a special place in my heart where, every time God looks at me (which is constantly, according to His Word), the first thing He has to see is her. This is one way we can pray endlessly—with an attitude, an awareness, and a constant inner holding up of a dear one.

Not all prayers have words. Some of our deepest petitions are groans, sighs, or tears salted with pain of identification. Some of our best prayers are the silent leaning of the soul in trust—in grateful knowledge that God is great, loving, and able. And some of our most effective prayers are poured out through active hands and feet, helping, carrying, lifting, and doing.

I have been and am being prayed for. So I know and count on the value and strength of prayer. Therefore, I pray for you.

With and without words, I hold you constantly before the Father, dear hurting one, precious lost one, beloved growing and struggling one, you who are exactly like me. To pray for you is both my obligation and my privilege.

Some day we'll know what prayer is really worth . . . and we'll deeply regret that we prayed so little.

But for now, we can be quite sure of this much: Our Father gathers our faithful, loving prayers and with such raw materials creates His marvelous answers.

> "As for me, far be it from me that I should sin against the Lord by failing to pray for you."   1 Samuel 12:23

I'm Not Good Enough!

Reality may stink sometimes, but then so does fertilizer.   S. L. L.

One of life's biggest discouragements has been the disparity between the high plain my soul cries out for and the valley where I generally plow my crooked furrows. Over the years I have often brought to the Lord my need to do better than I do and to be better than I am.

Surely nothing is wrong with my stretching for the best, with reaching toward the perfection that will be our inheritance some day. The danger lies in perfection*ism*—in not owning and enjoying my humanity—in striving and struggling so hard toward the goal that I mask the truth of who and what I am right now—in not always believing that God completely accepts me in this unfinished state—and in not understanding that it is from living in today's raw reality that I will grow.

God *does* accept us and reach out to embrace us in all-knowing love. Is this hard to believe? Do we somehow see Him demanding more, and frowning, shaking His head in disappointment, or withholding full love and approval until we measure up to His high and holy standards?

We had better take another look. If this is how we feel, it is not the true and loving God that we bow before, but a false idol, fashioned by harsh and impossible ideals imbedded deep within us.

We need to ask that the eyes of our heart be opened so that we can see who God really is. And we need to notice where He's standing. God is standing on our side!

It wasn't easy for Him to get to "our side." A steep and rugged hill called Calvary towered between us. But He made the climb . . . just so that He could open His arms there and accept us "as is."

He didn't go through all that only to change His mind later. He went through all that to help us to change. This is the God we can trust.

> But God demonstrates his own love for us in this: While we were still sinners, Christ died for us. . . . For if, when we were God's enemies, we were reconciled to him through the death of his Son, how much more, having been reconciled, shall we be saved through his life!　　Romans 5:8, 10

Sitting in Darkness

"When I sit in darkness, the *Lord* shall be a light unto me."   Micah 7:8 KJV

There is a place where the
> *wounded soul goes to hide,*
a place that cannot be reached
> *by human caring,*
though it nods at the effort.
> *It's a dark, retractable place,*
without windows and doors;
> *a place where the soul would be*
more alone than it has ever known
> *unless Someone—*
Someone able to walk through walls—
> *was not already there waiting.*

Though the doors were locked, Jesus came and stood among them and said, "Peace be with you!"   John 20:26

"Never will I leave you; never will I forsake you."   Hebrews 13:5

To Name a Fear

Who is more foolish, the child afraid of the dark, or the man afraid of the light?

Maurice Freehill

*T*he subject of my Tuesday morning women's Bible study class was "fear," and it was with a certain amount of fear that I faced the teaching of it. For I knew that I had to begin with a confession.

As I'd been preparing the lesson that week, I'd found myself reveling in the satisfaction that at least I'm not a fearful person. I've simply never wrestled with those vicious, debilitating lions of fear that I've seen roar through some people's lives, threatening to tear them apart.

It was just about then, I explained to the class, that our Lord poked His finger through the veneer of my smugness and pointed out that I've been calling my fear "Tabby," patting it on the head and feeding it saucers of milk for years!

How dangerous fear is when it purrs rather than roars. For then we don't recognize it as our enemy; and we invite it to curl up and stay on the hearth of our lives.

And while we claim we're not "afraid," we often find ourselves concerned, worried, restless, anxious, bored, frequently sick, unmotivated (or else working frantically); or we feel guilty, indecisive, possessive, negative, shy, or tired—oh, so tired!

It takes a brave person to admit, "I'm worried because I'm afraid you'll . . ." "I can't choose because I fear that if . . ." "I'm so tired from working hard to prevent . . ."

The masks of fear are many and varied. How they need to be uncovered and exposed to the Light of the World, Who says so often, "Fear not!" For He knows how many things in this world evoke fear in His children.

When we're ready to call our fears by their first name, we're ready to receive Jesus' antidote to fear—which is simply (or sometimes not so simply) the faith to trust in Him. He is able!

> "Do not be afraid. Stand firm and you will see the deliverance the Lord will bring you today. . . . The Lord will fight for you; you need only to be still."
>
> Exodus 14:13–14

Cultivating Joy

But the fruit of the Spirit is love, *joy . . .*   Galatians 5:22

We so often ask God
for joy
then are shocked when we
reap misery.
God plants joy eagerly,
yet it sprouts
only
in the rich soil of trust,
and it thrives
only
on the waters of
obedience and praise.
And it is true that
the tender seedling of
God's joy
and the stubborn weed of
self-pity
cannot survive in the same garden!

"If you obey my commands, you will remain in my love, just as I have obeyed my Father's commands and remain in his love. I have told you this so that my joy may be in you and that your joy may be complete."

John 15:10—11

For who is God besides the Lord? And who is the Rock except our God?
Psalm 18:31

I will say of the Lord, "He is my refuge and my fortress, my God, in whom I trust."
Psalm 91:2

Who Betrayed Whom?

"Stop trusting in man, who has but a breath in his nostrils."   Isaiah 2:22

I looked to you, my friend,
I trusted in you and
counted on your strength,
balance, and wisdom.
I believed in you!
Because you proved human,
because you fell,
does that make you a failure?
And does it mean I have been betrayed?
Or does it simply mean that I
heaped upon your slender shoulders
the burden of idealism—
that I placed you on the pedestal of
my high standards and
chained your feet with heavy links
of expectation?
Did I ask you to be God
and then weep when you were not?

Teen Trouble

Oh, to be only half as wonderful as my child thought I was when he was small, and only half as stupid as my teen-ager now thinks I am.

Rebecca Richards

Some days should never be recorded, repeated, or remembered. Take today, for instance. After a morning of upheaval with my daughter, she confided in me that she was in the absolute pits of a mood (she could have saved the trouble of making the announcement). Then she needed my complete attention for the next hour to gripe about everything and anything that has ever touched her nineteen-year-old world. She said she didn't know what's the matter with her lately, and I have a permanent crease across my tongue from resisting the urge to tell her!

She finally left for work, and my number-one son must have thought I'd be lonely for disaster, so he proceeded to erupt. He became incensed over some infraction to his personal sense of justice and shoved a bike at his brother, nearly wiping out his ability to father succeeding generations.

After tending to the offended, I tried to deal with the offender and got a verbal volley that could knock any mother off her Nikes. An impartial jury surely would have labeled it "mother abuse" and given him a few years in solitary.

So in the middle of this—I mean in the very middle of this scene, not knowing whether to laugh or to cry because this five-foot-ten-inch kid is exhibiting every characteristic of the "terrible twos" in outsized triplicate—a man called and asked if he had reached the Lenzkes residence . . . the Susan L. Lenzkes residence.

It seems he had discovered my book *When the Handwriting On the Wall Is in Brown Crayon* in, of all places, a doctor's waiting room, and he and his wife were so taken by it that they had headed straight for a bookstore and bought one.

At the bookstore they found out where I live. Then they found my phone number in the directory and called to tell me what a blessing my life was to them! (The Lord's timing is most humbling!)

But, I know that our Lord is faithful. He promised we could pick up snakes with our bare hands and drink deadly poison, *and live with teenagers* (well, that last addition seems to fit nicely here) and not be hurt at all!

Do not be far from me, for trouble is near and there is no one to help.
Psalm 22:11

The Gift of Laughter

I believe that laughter is a sacred sound to our God.   Tim Hansel

Not all laughter comes easily. There is a laughter that waits to be born. It is laughter at the end of exhaustion . . . laughter after pain . . . laughter for the joy of release . . . earned laughter . . . laughter all the brighter for its stark background . . . laughter stitched together with that ragged yet tough filament we call faith (or is it endurance?) . . . laughter that knows every note in the scale of life by heart—all its highs and lows—yet sings out its lilting tune anyway.

This laughter is more than just a sound, more than mirth, more than any comedian has ever hoped to evoke. It is the soul bubbling over with hope and victory. It is the voice of joy. Like a magnet it draws every scrap of life within its radius toward the promise of living, loving, and trusting.

Life does demand that we cry—often. But we need to laugh still more often. Because there will be an end to our tears but never to our joy!

"Blessed are you who weep now, for you will laugh."   Luke 6:21

Haven on Earth

S ometimes to suggest that we go to people for renewal is to suggest that we hop from one side of a searing pan to the other. Very often it's from humans that we need relief!

When our burden has been people, perhaps we need God's natural refreshment—solitude in His haven on earth.

> *God*
> *laces His thickets*
> *with solace,*
> *soaks His clouds*
> *with cleansing,*
> *arches His skies*
> *with protection,*
> *splashes His flowers*
> *with cheer,*
> *stirs His trees*
> *with a second wind,*

buoys His oceans
with assurance,
and heaps His mountains
with Hope—
'tis His haven of love,
His hint of heaven.

Ought we—the weary, the worn, the disconsolate—ignore such generosity?

For the Lord is the great God,
 the great King above all gods.
In his hand are the depths of the earth,
 and the mountain peaks belong to him.
The sea is his, for he made it,
 and his hands formed the dry land.
Come, let us bow down in worship,
 let us kneel before the Lord our Maker;
for he is our God
 and we are the people of his pasture,
the flock under his care.

           Psalm 95:3–7

A Lecture to Myself
at Pruning Season

"I am the true vine and my Father is the gardener. He cuts off every branch in me that bears no fruit, while every branch that does bear fruit he trims clean so that it will be even more fruitful."
John 15:1–2

*L*ook at you. What a restless branch you are—squirming, aching, offering suggestions, and protesting in the hands of your Lord!

Stop fighting! Stop trying so hard to understand it all, to make the changes, to know the direction and outcome of this pruning.

Rest. Just rest in Him. You know He can be trusted. So trust!

Trust enough to stop being His special assistant. He doesn't really need the help.

Trust enough to let yourself cry for what is and what isn't. Trust enough to praise and thank your Vine for what is and what will be.

Trust enough to take a *nap*, for goodness' sake!

No discipline seems pleasant at the time, but painful. Later on, however, it produces a harvest of righteousness and peace for those who have been trained by it.
Hebrews 12:11

115

The Morning of Eternity

"See, I have engraved you on the palms of my hands."   Isaiah 49:16

*T*here are probably no clouds more threatening than those that gathered above Christ's tortured cross. All of creation must have rushed to black mourning for the shame of it—that their Creator, the One whose hand formed the earth and heavens, should have those hands pierced with the nails of our sin!

But deep inside the cloud's darkness, lightning glory gathered, waiting to burst forth in victory, waiting to split the dark veil of sin hung between God and His beloved mankind.

Has ever such a silver lining been spoken as, "It is finished"?

Perhaps only, "He is risen!"

Oh, world, trace with joy the silver lining that will never tarnish. Tell it everywhere—

RISEN!

is

He

"He is not here; he has risen, just as he said."   Matthew 28:6

117

PART IV

*Through
the Dark Times
God Wants Us
to Grow*

Growing Pains

Growing up isn't for sissies. Mary Betcher

*T*he difficult truth about truth is that if often requires change . . . in us, in our perspectives, attitudes, and rules for living.

Change of any sort is rarely easy. Change that produces progress in personal growth is never easy. Yet as we submit to the One Who never changes, He marvelously works in our lives.

I have a friend rich in the determination and honesty that personal growth requires. She is rich too in opportunities, for life dealt her a crushing load—one that offered the unyielding choices of "fight" or "fold." She chose to fight and invited me to join her.

As I walked with this friend through her struggles, I occasionally heard her wail, "Please, Lord, I don't want to grow anymore!"

But I happen to know that she didn't really mean it. For other than unscheduled retreats beneath the covers of her bed for tears and talk with the Lord, she has never stopped enlarging the house of her spirit; she has never stopped rebuilding the losses of her incredibly painful childhood and early adulthood; she has never stopped seeking to know and be known, love and be loved; she has never stopped discovering her worth and potential; and she has never stopped choosing to let go of the wounds in order to free her hands for living and for a ministry of real understanding to other wounded ones.

121

It's the pain of such continuous stretching effort that my friend bemoans. And I can't blame her, for I too know that growing pains are real, that they puncture our energy level and cut through our reserves.

Neither can I blame her for not fully appreciating her progress, for she doesn't have the beautiful view of the results that I have. I have always hoped, though, that she could hear applause in my words and see approval mirrored in my love. For growing up is the hardest, most important, and most courageous work that we'll ever do.

Speaking the truth in love, we will in all things grow up into him who is the Head, that is, Christ.   Ephesians 4:15

You Are Precious

As a teacher teaches best by sparking curiosity, so an encourager encourages best by kindling self-worth.   S.L.L.

*T*he deepest trough of discouragement is worthlessness. It's easy to imagine that we deserve our ditches of despair, so why hope, why try? Arms shortened with self-negation cannot stretch for help unless help comes very near.

When help comes near through one of God's loving children, it begins with listening and ends with lifting. For if a listening ear is the best instrument of an encourager, it is only because it plays the melody of love that sings out, "You're worth my time, worth my attention, uniquely worthy of not only *my* caring but also *God's.*"

Paul instructs us to observe whatever is true, noble, right, pure, lovely, admirable, excellent, and praiseworthy (Phil. 4:8). As the encourager sees and affirms these qualities in others those who are disheartened begin to see the *Source* of all that is true and excellent and praiseworthy. And soon they begin praising their lovely Creator by becoming all He meant for them to be.

"I have called you by name; you are mine. . . . You are precious and honored in my sight . . . I love you."   Isaiah 43: 1—4

Soaring in His Image

And God said, ". . . let birds fly above the earth across the expanse of the
sky." . . . Then God said, "Let us make man in our image, in our likeness"
. . . God saw all that he had made, and it was very good.

Genesis 1:20, 26, 31

*E*very day I watch hawks sweeping through the canyon outside my window,
taking advantage of invisible hills and valleys of wind, gliding and soaring.
How magnificent they are! How true to their Creator's intention!

And I find myself praying out deep longings as I watch them. "Make me be that
free and alive, Father. Help me not to scurry about the underbrush of this world while
currents and wings wait empty. Do I waste such beauty when I huddle or crawl? Do I
play rodent and burrow, hiding and hoarding meager strivings?

"You offer me so much—so much mercy for sin, so much grace for living, so
much power in weakness. What is the untested wingspan of Your purpose in me?

"Oh Lord, if I do nothing else in my life, may I at least honor You by being,
doing, and enjoying what You created me to be, do, and enjoy. Let me *soar!*"

"He gives strength to the weary and increases the power of the weak . . .
They will soar on wings like eagles . . ."

Isaiah 40:29, 31

What a Life

My grandfather always said that living is like licking honey off a thorn.
Louis Adamic

*L*ife is sweet. It offers sunrises, fat baby fists, darting hummingbirds, commitments, outstretched arms, spring breezes, puppies, giggles, strawberries, voices in harmony, dimples, sheets on a clothesline, curls on little girls, compliments, fresh-baked bread, red wagons, great oak trees, whiskered men, love letters, pink parasols, marching bands, harvest time, feather pillows, waterfalls, boys and bikes, praise songs, full moons, communion, reunion, daisies, helping hands, pounding surf, butterflies, and white clouds mounded in blue skies.

Life is sharp. It pierces with goodbyes, fevered brows, screams, empty beds, tornados, prejudice, poison ivy, tear-stained cheeks, ignorance, war, failure, drought, explosions, greed, broken bones, broken promises, broken dreams, broken hearts, broken lives, criticism, head-on collisions, rust and rot, floods, doubts, rejection, wrinkles, mosquitoes, hunger, hands that slap or take, despair, divorce, rape, depression, and dark clouds mounded in gray skies.

How can we fit it all together? How can we embrace the sweet joys of life without being stabbed by its jagged thorns? We cannot. There is no way to withdraw from only part of life.

127

We're told that because of God's enemy and our sinful choice, the wheat and weeds are sown together in this world. Our job is to stand firm and grow where we are planted by using all the sunshine and rain that comes our way. Would we come to harvest without either?

". . . while you are pulling the weeds, you may root up the wheat with them. Let both grow together until the harvest. At that time I will tell the harvesters: First collect the weeds and tie them in bundles to be burned, then gather the wheat and bring it into my barn."   Matthew 13:29−30

God's Exchange System

To all who mourn . . . he will give: Beauty for ashes; Joy instead of mourning; Praise instead of heaviness.   Isaiah 61:3 LB

Whenever we bow in real understanding before our Lord—whether it's at the cradle, the cross, or the empty tomb; whether we're seeing Him as Savior, Friend, or conquering King—we find ourselves longing to give Him some wonderful, worthy gift. The Eastern Wise Men, at least, brought gold, frankincense, and myrrh!

But we know how it is, how it's always been. We come to Him dressed in the rags of sin—and He gives to us His robe of righteousness. We offer our empty, wounded broken hearts—and He fills them with love, and life, and healing.

We bring Him needs—He supplies His endless resources. We give tears—He gives comfort. We give weakness—He gives grace. We cry out our fears and questions—He whispers His peace and purpose. We present ignorance wrapped in pride—He returns wisdom wrapped in humility.

He knows how it is, how it's always been, and yet He pleads with us to continue to come to Him and give all that we are and all that we are not.

Because He knows something else. He knows that when we have finally given Him all that we are and have *received all that He is*, we will at last hold the One Gift worth giving back to Him.

Our gold is surrender; our frankincense, praise; our myrrh, obedience. Worthy gifts in His gracious eyes.

"I have neither silver nor gold, but I will give you what I have." Acts 3:6 MLB

Who's Hurting Now?

Have I shed more tears for God's pain or for mine?   S. L. L.

When life is difficult, we might try setting aside our own pain and ask, rather, to know what hurts God. Does it pain Him that His children know light, yet so often turn toward darkness? That He fits us with the spectacles of His heavenly view, yet we grope on in myopia? That He offers uncommon guidance, and we follow common sense? That He is *the* Way, and we take *a* way?

Is His frustration that He spreads the banquet of His love, yet we feed on the dry crumbs of doubt and self-negation? That He offers power to move mountains, and we stumble over mole hills? That He delivers us from evil, and we wink at His Enemy? That we cling to Him in pain, then wave to Him in ease? That He presents peace, and we battle our way toward it? That He brought salvation to all, and we hoard it as a private joy? Perhaps it hurts Him most that we casually call Him "Lord, Lord," when we need first to be on our knees crying, "Savior, Savior!" He waits to help in our weaknesses, sins, and failings. He already shared *our* pain. As we begin to understand, share, and agree with what hurts *Him*, growth begins.

> God looks down from heaven on the sons of men to see if there are any
> who understand, any who seek God.   Psalm 53:2

Choices

"Small is the gate and narrow the road that leads to life." Matthew 7:14

Which of us doesn't own a clear mental picture of the "straight and narrow way"? After all, it's self-descriptive.

We begin by defining its entrance, so tightly drawn with the restrictions of holiness that one must kneel in surrender to enter, for only Jesus Christ, Son of God, could open the way.

From this gateway, we imagine a neat path that stretches like a slender, ribboned highway—arrow straight and uninterrupted from here to eternity. But something bothers me about this neat one-lane road. Real life offers more avenues of choice than allowed by the rigid borders of this long-standing image.

I need to change my perception of the straight-and-narrow road. Instead of a smooth, uninterrupted path, I see many crossroads, for my declared decision to follow Christ has been regularly intersected and tested with four-way stops and offers of alternate routes.

The glaring signposts at these junctions point to glittering cities of desire or offer a comfortable oasis from difficulty. Some suggest alternative attitudes toward God, myself, others, and life. Other signs, worn and faded, make the difference between good and best almost indiscernible. Does it really matter which career, friends, or lifestyle I choose? Does this small moment—this small choice—matter?

133

It matters. This straight road with its myriad intersections requires the constant map of God's Word, as well as unfaltering attention to our faithful companion and guide, Jesus Christ.

The name of the road we travel is, "Follow Me." This is our constant choice.

This is what the Lord says: "Stand at the crossroads and look; ask for the ancient paths, ask where the good way is, and walk in it, and you will find rest for your souls. . . ."
                                                                    Jeremiah 6:16

Don't Give Up!

By perseverance the snails reached the ark.   Charles Hadden Spurgeon

W e're slow-brew Christians in an instant world. Small wonder that we get discouraged with ourselves!

The world serves up instant food, instant entertainment, and instant credit. We're offered computers, microwave ovens, automatic phone dialers, remote control televisions, polaroid cameras, high-speed elevators, and quick copy machines. We can reach for hot-line help, rapid-rise yeast, express mail, and automatic banking. We can travel in racy cars with high-octane fuel, supersonic jets, and even orbit the globe in space capsules.

Then comes the Christian—a foot soldier on a straight and narrow path. "Follow Me," Jesus says. "Put one foot in front of the other in moment-to-moment obedience." (Nothing like an invitation to take a stroll on the freeway!)

Then Jesus tells us He's going to make us "fishers of men." What? Bait and wait? Mend and cast nets? Clean and preserve the catch? (An unattractive assignment when we have fillet of fish divan in the frozen food sections of our modern supermarkets!)

Next we discover that we're required to "bear much fruit." And fruit, we realize with a groan, is the end product of a seed—with a slow-growing tree in between!

135

So we're not surprised to find that we're instructed to "grow up into Him Who is the Head." Growing up is the slowest thing that happens to a child . . . even slower than waiting for Christmas. And eagerness adds neither an inch to the stature nor a year to the calendar.

Growth isn't fast, yet it does yield high gains all along the path to eternity. In His Word our Lord explains to us, "You know that the testing of your faith develops perseverance. Perseverance must finish its work so that you may be mature and complete, not lacking anything" (James 1:3–4).

Still, it might help our patience and perseverance to realize that while there are no instant formulas for us on this earth, God has the most glorious "instant" of all prepared for His children!

But we will all be changed—in a flash, in the twinkling of an eye, at the last trumpet. For the trumpet will sound, the dead will be raised imperishable, and we will be changed.   2 Corinthians 15:51–52

Walking and Waiting

Waiting on the Lord affords us our finest progress.   S.L.L.

Sometimes we're certain we're going nowhere in life. We find ourselves trapped between the walls of some narrow, spartan place, which we wrongly conclude must be one of life's dreary waiting rooms. So we sit down, reach for an outdated periodical, and wait for someone to open a door and call our name.

I'm afraid many of us who think we are being patient are camping in life's *hallways!* Our Lord's house has many rooms, and how can we get from one to another except through a hallway? Yes, some are long, some narrow, some dark, and some barren. Yet if we fail to understand the purpose of a hallway, we're likely to wander about for years, piously claiming to be "waiting on the Lord."

Although life's hallways *are* times of waiting, they are also times of moving forward toward exciting new rooms of potential, maturity, and service. We can trust Him to bring us to the next open door in His perfect time—the time that will most benefit us and the glory of His name.

Let's practice waiting on the Lord even as we faithfully walk the narrow way.

But one thing I do: Forgetting what is behind and straining toward what is ahead, I press on toward the goal. . . .   Philippians 3:13–14

Blessed are the flexible.

David Kidron

Flexible Living

Stiffen your neck no more.   Deuteronomy 10:16 NASB

*M*any of us are crippled from birth. The backbone of our standard for living comes fused into unyielding rules and regulations. We are rigid in our determination to control life's course and outcome.

We're sure, for example, how people ought to look, behave, and respond. Things have to be done a certain way—our way. We know, too, exactly how a godly marriage should operate; and we're quite familiar with the model of the ideal Christian family scene—which, of course, we intend to duplicate perfectly.

Then real life sneaks up and whacks us from behind, seeking to break our unbending back and our stiff neck, threatening to paralyze us.

There is a cure. We are offered opportunity to exercise the suppleness of godly grace and perspective. Each time life throws us a punch, we can do a deep knee bend, forcing our muscles of faith, hope, and understanding to stretch.

Eventually that brittle backbone will grow strong and supple, bending with the rhythms of grace yet standing tall and firm in the face of compromise.

All of this requires considerable daily "give." Such give is not a one-time choice but a lifestyle of generosity, spontaneity, and openness to truth.

How often I have thought that if I could give just one gift to my children— besides a heart for God—it would be the golden gift of flexibility.

A Safe Place

To be a "safe place" for others, I must have an open heart and a closed mouth.

S. L. L.

I have a friend who has managed to pave between the two of us a broad welcoming place where I can run to think new and uncertain thoughts and test unfamiliar feelings—a place where I can wander until I'm ready to run in confidence.

Having come often to this cherished "safe place," bordered only by the embrace of acceptance, I realize that there is no more precious gift than this gift of understanding.

This friend has been a mirror, steadily and clearly reflecting who, what, and where I am in my journey through life. And I have been "paralleled"—joined, though never intruded upon—in this journey of discovery and growth.

When I thank God for His rich goodness toward me, I thank Him for this friend. And when I ask God to make me like His Son Jesus and to use me in His kingdom and for His glory, I feel Him making me into a safe place, an understanding place, a steady, warm, non-judgmental, and, oh yes, a leakproof place—like this friend.

"Each man will be like a shelter from the wind and a refuge from the storm, like streams of water in the desert and the shadow of a great rock in a thirsty land."   Isaiah 32:2

The Failure of Failing

We all stumble in many ways.   James 3:2

S ome of life's clouds manage to stay high above us and merely threaten. Some sprinkle or mist, and some pour torrents. Other clouds move right down to where we live and settle upon our most unprotected core, our self-esteem.

One such cloud is the leaden fogbank of personal failure. It rolls over our souls, a damp blanket of self-deprecation, depressing us and often obscuring our judgment. Soon we are in danger of believing not that we have *failed* but that we are a *failure*. What difference between the two!

To have *failed* is to have lived, tried, and been proven to be imperfect like everyone else. To have failed is to own more wisdom, understanding, and experience than do those who sit on life's sidelines, playing it safe. To have failed is to claim a clearer knowledge of what not to do the next time. And to have failed is to extend to ourselves the grace that God extends to us.

We become a *failure* when we allow a mistake to swallow our ability to learn, give, grow, and try again. We become a failure if we let the "shoulds" and the "if onlys" suck us into their inextricable mire. We become a failure also if we become content with failing.

Blunders, errors, and failures can become quicksand traps of regret, or they can be building blocks of regeneration. The choice is ours.

Resurrecting Dreams

The word of God is living and active. Sharper than any double-edged sword, it penetrates to dividing soul and spirit, joints and marrow; it judges the thoughts and attitudes of the heart. Nothing in all creation is hidden from God's sight. Everything is uncovered and laid bare before the eyes of him to whom we must give account.   Hebrews 4:12–13

*T*he Lord has a way of looking through the magnifying glass of His Word into the very heart of things—especially the human heart. And there's no use trying to hide what's there.

One day I came to His Word with a nameless ache tucked away inside, troubling me, as it had been for several days. I read Luke's account of Jesus entering the town of Nain, where He came upon a heartbroken widow following the coffin of her only son.

When the Lord saw her, his heart went out to her and he said, "Don't cry." Then he went up and touched the coffin, and those carrying it stood still. He said, "Young man, I say to you, get up!" The dead man sat up and began to talk, and Jesus gave him back to his mother.   Luke 7:13–15

As I pondered what this story could possibly have to do with me, the Lord looked into this mother's heart and said, "Something has died in you, Susan. What is this thing you're mourning and carrying in a coffin?"

I was startled, for I hadn't known that a funeral was going on inside me. But He reached out and touched the coffin that I was, indeed, laboring beneath, and I finally stood still and looked.

An important dream was being taken for burial—a dream the Lord knew I needed to have alive.

Very quietly, from within the depths of me I heard Jesus whisper, "Do you suppose that if I can resurrect people, I can resurrect dreams, too?"

"Yes, Lord! Let's get on with life. Make me a place of miracle—a miracle of faith, perseverance, and rejoicing in hope. I want to celebrate more than I want to mourn!"

I have set before you life and death, blessings and curses. Now choose life,
so that you and your children may live and that you may love the Lord your
God, listen to his voice, and hold fast to him. For the Lord is your life. . . .
Deuteronomy 30:19–20

A Harvest of Thanksgiving

Thanksgiving was never meant to be shut up in a single day.
Robert Caspar Lintner

Our Pilgrim parents knew hardship, stark poverty, sickness, despair, and loss upon loss as they were pitted against hostile nature. A combination of exposure, over-exertion, and inadequate provisions claimed one brave life after another. An entry in the Pilgrims' records starkly sums up their tragedy:

> March 21, 1621, "This month thirteen of our company die. And in the three months past dies half of our company . . . Of a hundred persons—scarce fifty remain . . . the living scarcely able to bury the dead."

Yet one by one they carried their precious ones to a field at the summit of a small cliff and buried them there—thirteen of the eighteen wives, more than half of the fathers, four entire families.

Realizing that the Indians must not be allowed to know the extent of their losses, they did not mark the graves with even a small stone. Instead they planted over their grave-field with corn.

We are not suffering as our Pilgrim parents did, yet we are still afflicted today.

146

Some of us have not yet laid aside our shovels of loss, damp with the dirt of despair from burying what was most precious to us—people, cherished hopes, dreams.

Our Enemy is watching. Can we be as brave as our ancestors and baffle the Enemy by refusing even to mark the graves of our losses? More than that, dare we convert our cemeteries to cornfields?

Ah, that we may learn to yield a harvest of Thanksgiving from the ground of our losses! It is our rich heritage!

Let us continually offer to God a sacrifice of praise.   Hebrews 13:15

A Tribute to Living

Some die without having lived; others live, though they have already
died.   Unknown

To My Dear Pastor Hart,

I'm forwarding this letter to your heavenly address. Even though you are gone, I
need to tell you some things. I want you to know the most important lessons you taught
me, both from the pulpit and from your life.

You proved to me that life is best lived in precise, declarative sentences of truth.
That such truth delivers best when it is both simple and profound. That truth belabored
is truth belittled. I experienced the impact of this truth as you mixed it with humor,
enthusiasm, love, commitment, and full knowledge of its authority.

I watched you prove that people, God's Word, and His presence, praise, and
love are the only important and lasting things on this earth.

I watched you savor and enjoy all that God brought to you while you were here.
I have never known anyone more fully alive while confined to the limitations of humanity
and this world.

But God has taken you home now, and you are truly alive. He has left me here.
I will carry on.

You left rich resources for the task, for I've not only been taught but also
touched and changed by you. I feel the stinging pressure of the truth that life is short. I

feel the challenge of the truth that my world will not be changed unless I spend myself as you did.

You were a good steward of your life—you spent it for the glory of God. I, in turn, will try to be a good steward of your death, spending its opportunities also for the glory of God.

But I can't help missing you. I'm not ashamed of my tears. I'm so grateful that I told you, just two days before you left us so unexpectedly, that I love you and thank God for bringing you to us. You, in turn, told me how much you loved me—loved us all—and how thankful you were that you came here.

You did, indeed, love us. How well named you were. You both lived and died with heart.

God gave us His best in you. I'll not waste His generous gift.

Eternal love in Christ,
Susan

"He has crossed over from death to life."   John 5:24

[Written on the death of my pastor, Hartley Christenson, who suffered a massive heart attack while playing tennis on September 7, 1985, at the age of 49.]

He Comes in Winter

Oh, that you would rend the heavens and come down! . . .   Isaiah 64:1

He could have come in
        springtime
                when flowers force their way
through sod and
                bleating hope is born.
He could have been spring's Lamb!

He could have come in
        summer
                when sun streams down
to warm that hope and
                breezes cool the doubts.
Ho, summer's Brightest Son!

He could have come in
        autumn
                when hope flames forth
with blazing joy and
                crimson paints the earth.
Behold, He's autumn's Glory!

151

But He comes in
          winter
                    when hope lies frozen
          in the night and
                    blizzards rake our souls.
He comes, our Living Hope!

"I came that they may have life, and have it abundantly."   John 10:10 RSV

Today Is Tomorrow

Is not what I shall be capable of tomorrow contained in what I am today?

Paul Tournier

Let's get started on tomorrow.
Let's reach out
through each day's clouds or sunshine and
> *shape our hopes,*
> *shift our losses,*
> *learn our lessons,*
> *touch our purpose,*
> *taste our potential,*
> *and claim our inheritance in Christ.*
Let's get started on tomorrow by
living fully and gratefully
this day.
Each day, well lived,
peeks around the curtain and effortlessly
pre-arranges tomorrow.

"Do not be anxious about tomorrow, for tomorrow will be anxious for itself."

Matthew 6:34 RSV

Epilogue

It's funny how life sometimes draws its own conclusions. As I worked on the final edited copy of this book about cloudy days, I witnessed the most fascinating succession of storms that we've experienced during our nine years in San Diego.

Last week a front-page headline in our newspaper announced, "Storm, sun tussle for San Diego skies." The sun had her shining moments, but as an unbiased "weather referee," I declare the storm the undisputed winner of the weeklong tussle. The rain paraded a dozen personalities a day—pouring, pelting, driving, sprinkling, sheeting, hailing, misting, and splattering—stepping aside only at brief intervals to let the sun wink its false promise.

As I sat at the table working on revisions late one night, the rain began to drive in cold needles against the dark windows. Driven by ruthless bursts of wind, it smeared and scooted across the window panes. Although I was wrapped snugly in a warm woolen blanket, I found myself shivering. The rain seemed to hammer against my soul with the chilling knowledge that people are actually outdoors in such storms. Perhaps you.

I began praying for you, not knowing your name but feeling the terrible shiver of your need for shelter and warmth. I prayed that this book would somehow warm you, help you, and lead you to the shelter of The Most High.

I prayed also for those of us who sit by our cozy fireplaces refusing to look outside where you are. And I prayed for those of us out there with you who have only our own little umbrella to share. I prayed that each of us would become "a shelter from the wind and a refuge from the storm" (Isaiah 32:2).

Photo Credits

E. Martene Craig
12, 16, 20, 30, 40, 86, 88, 106,
112, 118, 120, 126, 136, 141, 142

Peter Essau
124

Herb Lenzkes
36, 46, 52, 59, 70, 78, 84,
94, 105, 108, 116, 132, 138

Bob Miller
148, 152